TECHNIQUES

OF

BEADING

EARRINGS

by

DEON
DELANGE

Eagle's View Publishing
6756 N. North Fork Rd.
Liberty, Utah 84310

Library of Congress Card Number: 83-82121
ISBN 0-943604-03-6

* * * * * * * * * * *

DEDICATION

To Margaret Coffey, for sharing part of her
culture with me and helping to start a dream. To
my daughter, Yvette, who helped fulfill the dream.
And, to my family and friends without whose
encouragement, this dream would not have come true.

Contents

ABOUT THE AUTHOR

Deon has been making and creating beaded earrings and necklaces for twelve years and has won a number of awards at state fairs, pow wows and craft shows. What started as a personal interest has developed into a family enterprise that now employees Deon, her husband Don and her two children. Her daughter, Yvette, when only eleven years old, starting winning awards for her creative earring designs.

Born in Salt Lake City, Utah, Deon cultivated her talent in the northwest. In 1982 the family decided to make craftwork a full-time vocation, purchased a trailer and started "on the road" making and selling these beautiful earrings.

* * * * * * * * * * * *

ACKNOWLEDGMENTS

While only the author can be held responsible for mistakes and omissions, there are a number of people who have been instrumental in the creation of this book. First and foremost, my editor, Monte Smith, who was not only the driving force in getting the book completed but also added ideas, depth and his photographic talents. Monte Smith, Jr. assisted in designing the book and supplied the graphics and illustrations. Christine Christopher "proof-read" the manuscript a number of times and made many valuable suggestions. And most important of all my mother for her continued support and my husband and children whose encouragement made this all possible.

Introduction

Every attempt has been made to make this book easy and enjoyable to use. Following the Introduction are complete instructions on making Deon's Designs Originale Earrings. This is followed by graphed designs and variations and these start with the easiest earrings and progress to the more difficult designs. There is then a description of how to make necklaces and necklace chains and then how to make other types of earrings and their variations. The last section is about using graph paper and designing original earrings.

Making earrings and necklaces with beads is enjoyable and creative. There are, however, a few things to keep in mind that will help make beading easier and will also be helpful in using this book.

(1) Be selective in choosing beads of uniform size. This is very important in this kind of beadwork in order to obtain a pleasing, over-all appearance and to insure uniformity in design. The most uniform beads are available from Indian craft supply houses and are purchased in bunches called "hanks." When buying the beads, it is important to place all of the colors to be used side by side and insure that all of the beads are uniform. Each hank, however, will have a number of beads that have weird shapes or are slightly larger or smaller than the others and these should be discarded as the beading is done. If it is necessary to purchase the beads in containers, be very selective when beading to choose uniform beads.

(2) When making any of the earrings that have both bugle beads and seed beads, the size of the bugle bead determines what size seed bead to use. Therefore, **a size 3/° bugle bead may be used with size 11/° or 12/° seed beads, but a size 2/° may be used with only size 12/° seed beads or** smaller. As in all glass Czechoslovakian seed

beads, the larger the number the smaller the bead.

(3) Keep the beads in separate containers or jars. This will make finding the needed color and size bead easier and will insure that different sizes do not get mixed. For future work, it may be advisable to not only label the size and color on the containers, but also the color number and where they were purchased. Most craft supply houses have their own color numbers and this will make reordering easier.

(4) Be sure you have enough beads of the proper colors to finish your project before beginning. Bead colors will vary in shade from dye batch to dye batch and it is often impossible to find the right shade when a project is half complete.

(5) When beading, use a felt covered desk blotter or a piece of styrofoam that has been covered with fabric. It is best to have a work area that is comfortable to work on and that will not allow the beads to roll away. As the beading is done, the different colors and sizes of beads should be kept in separate piles, or in different saucers (white is the best color), or trays, or they may be taken directly from the hank strings. The idea is to be able to select uniform beads as you work, so try different methods to find the one that works best.

(6) The best needles for this kind of work are made in England and are Size 15/° Beading Needles. If these are unavailable, a size 16/° Japanese beading needle can be used, but these are generally more brittle, larger and less convenient to use.

(7) The best thread to use is "Nymo" (made of nylon), in a size "A" or "0."

(8) Always work in a well lighted room. It may be that a clamp-on elbow lamp or a desk lamp with an adjustable neck will be helpful. However, flouorescent lighting is not suggested, as it tends to alter the color of some beads.

(9) A pair of small pointed, sharp craft scissors will be very helpful. When cutting the thread from a finished piece of beadwork, lay the scissor blades flat against the beadwork and then clip carefully close to the work. Clipping the threads with just the tips of the blades at an angle could cut threads that are part of the beadwork that should not be cut.

(10) When making necklace and earring sets, try to use complimentary designs that show a relationship between the two. A necklace using floral designs will compliment earrings if they also have similar floral designs, etc.

(11) It is suggested that the beginner use small and simple designs to begin, then progress to larger and more difficult pieces. Making several pairs of earrings in the beginning will help keep away from frustration and mistakes that can occur with larger work.

(12) Please read the complete procedure before beginning the beadwork so that you will have a more complete understanding of the technique.

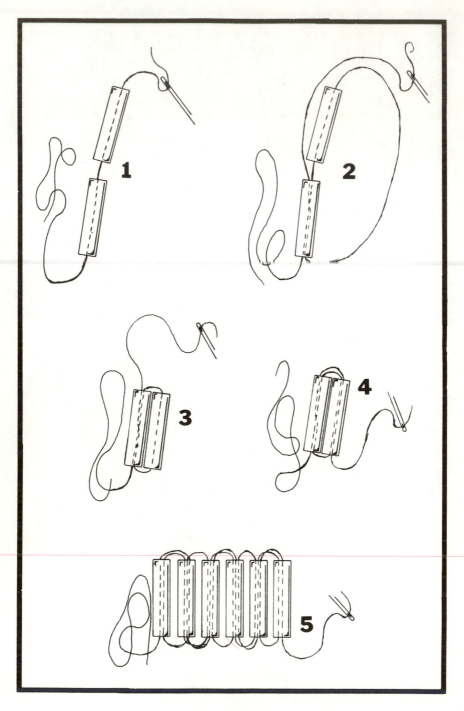

Deon's Designs
Originale Earrings

All of the earrings in this first section may be made with the following recommended materials:

    1 bobbin "nymo" thread size A or O
    1 package 15/° beading needles
    1 pair small sharp scissors
    1 hank bugle beads - either size 3/°
       or 2/°*
    1 hank seed beads - either size 11/°
       or 12/°*
    1 hank contrasting color seed beads -
       either size 11/° or 12/°*
    ----
    * - see "Introduction" for correct
    combination of seed and bugle beads.

The **Bugle Beads** are the foundation for this type of beadwork and serve as a starting point. The number of bugle beads contained in the foundation will determine the width of the finished piece, and will also resolve the overall size of the piece.

- - PHASE I - -

This phase will form the foundation row of bugle beads that the rest of the piece is attached to. Refer to one of the charted graphs that follow this section and count the number of bugle beads in the chosen design. Join them as follows:
STEP 1 - Using a single thread (just over two (2) yards long for an earring six (6) bugle beads wide), place two (2) bugle beads on the thread and push them to within 6-8" of the end (leave enough thread to tie off later), as shown in Figure 1.
Holding the short thread down, make a clock-

9

wise circle with the needle and go "up" through the first bugle bead following the direction of the thread (Figure 2). Pull the thread tight, and the two bugle beads will come together parallel with each other (Figure 3).

The needle will now be coming "up" through the first bugle bead. Complete this step by placing the needle "down" through the second bead (Figure 4).

STEP 2 - Continue adding bugle beads, one at a time, following the procedure described above and shown in Figures 2 through 4.

You will notice that there is a rhythm to this procedure as it progresses. The thread will go in a clockwise direction and then in a counter-clockwise direction, then clockwise again, etc.

As bugle beads are added, make sure that the thread is coming either up through, or down through the last bugle bead, depending upon the direction the thread is going. This can be simplified by **always** keeping the short "beginning" thread facing toward the left and downward (Figure 5). This will help lessen any confusion and assist in keeping the proper place.

When the beading thread is in the last bugle bead strung, pick up another bugle bead and, following the course of the thread, go either up through or down through the last attached bugle. For example, if there are two (2) bugle beads attached, the thread will be coming down through bugle number 2. Put bugle number 3 on the needle and go back down through bugle number 2. Now go up through bugle 3. Put on bugle #4 and follow the thread by going back up through bugle #3, then down through bugle 4, etc.

As shown in Figure 5, the rhythm for a six (6) bugle bead-wide piece will be: Bugles #1 and #2 on thread (with short thread to the left and pointing down), then up through #1, down through #2 and add number 3; down through #2, then up through #3 and add number 4; up through #3, then down through #4 and add number 5; down through #4, then up through #5 and add number 6; up through #5 and down through number 6.

With all six bugles in place, **work your way back across the bugles to reinforce them.** This is done by going up through #5, down through #4, up through #3, down through #2 and up through #1.

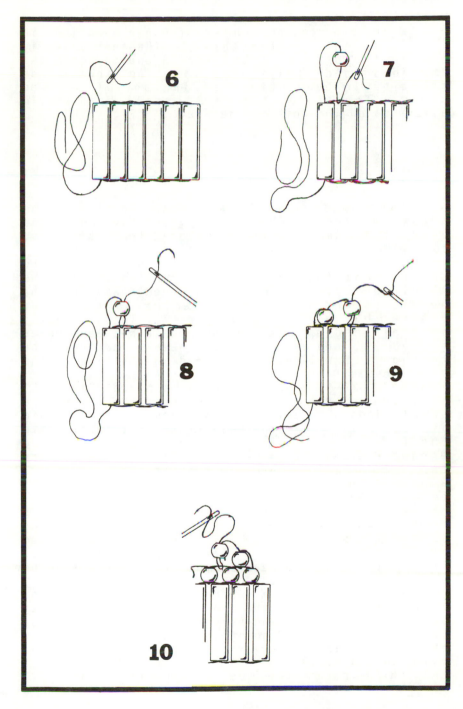

When the required number of bugle beads are in place, **do not cut the thread.** The next phase is the upper portion of the earing and to begin **the thread should always be coming "up" through the first bugle bead** before adding any of the seed beads. Therefore, **the first small bead should always be on the left of the piece.** (Fig. 6)

- - PHASE II - -

This phase will form the top portion of the beadwork piece. It is accomplished by adding one bead at a time to the bugle bead foundation just completed.

STEP 1 - Following the design on anyone of the charts that follow these instructions, place the required color of bead on the needle and pass the needle toward you, under the thread that goes between bugle #1 and #2 (Figure 7). This is easily accomplished by pushing the needle between bugles #1 and #2, and by pulling the needle and thread on through, it will place the bead in position on top of the bugles.

STEP 2 - To lock the bead in place (Figure 8) pass the needle up through the bead. Make sure the needle does not pass under the span of thread again as this will remove the bead from the thread. With the first bead in place, put the second bead on the thread and pass the needle under the thread between the second and third bugle bead as shown in Figure 9. Then bring the needle and thread up through this bead and lock it into place.

Continue this procedure (following the colors on the charts), beading on the first row of beads from LEFT to RIGHT. With the first row of seed beads in place, the needle and thread will be coming up from the bead on the far right. Move up one row on the charted designs to the bead directly above the row just finished. Now following from RIGHT to LEFT, place the proper color beads, one at a time, on the thread using the same procedure as the preceding row, **going under the thread between the seed beads,** rather than the bugles beads as shown in Figure 10.

The work on the seed bead portion (Phase II)

will continue in a LEFT to RIGHT, then RIGHT to
LEFT, then LEFT to RIGHT, etc., manner. As this
proceeds there will be one less bead in each row
you add. Also, the first row of beads will have one
less bead than the bugle bead row (See Figure 11).
Therefore, an earring containing seven (7) bugle
beads in the foundation row (Phase I), will have
six (6) seed beads in the first row, five (5) beads
in the next row, four (4) beads in row Three, three
(3) beads in the next row, and two (2) seed beads
in the fifth, or top, row. As the beading is done
in this phase, it is easy to see why it is very
important to use beads that are all the same, exact
size.

STEP 3 - When the row having only two beads
has been put in place, it is time to add the hanging loop: After locking the last bead in place on
the top row, the thread will be coming up out of
the bead on the right side in this example of seven
bugle beads wide. However, using an even number of
bugle beads will result in ending with the thread
on the left side.. As shown in Figure 12, place an
even number of beads on the thread (approximately
six (6) beads for earrings), go through these beads
again and then take the needle down through the
other bead on the two-bead, or top, row. Now pull
the loop next to the top row.

In larger earrings, as the loop that has been
formed will support the piece, work the thread
through the same beads again (including the beads
in the loop). This will add strength.

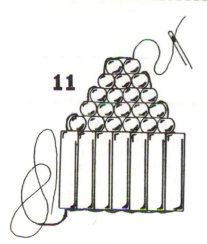

11

12

PHASE III

In this phase the bead dangles will be put in place at the bottom of the beadwork piece.

To do this, work the thread, diagonally, down through the beads to the bugle bead at the starting point as shown in Figure 13. With the thread down through the first bugle bead on the left, place the appropriate number and colors of seed beads on the thread (following the chart for the correct number and colors). Add one bugle bead at the bottom of the dangle, as indicated on the charts, and add three (3) seed beads. With the exception of these last three seed beads, pass the needle back up through all of the beads on the dangle; then push the needle back up through the first bugle on the foundation (Phase I) row as shown in Figure 14.

Adjust the dangle so that it will hang properly by placing a finger tip over the center bead of the three beads at the bottom of the dangle. By pulling the thread, adjust the dangle so that it hangs properly without too much or too little tension. As the work progresses, it is possible to feel the proper amount of tension.

To progress to the next dangle, pass the needle down through the next bugle bead on the foundation row (bugle bead #2), and add the next beaded dangle following the chart for color and number of beads.

Continue this process until all of the dangles are in place. Make sure that each has been properly adjusted so that they all hang with the same amount of tension.

PHASE IV

As shown in Figure 15, when the dangles have been put in place tie the thread off between two of the rows of seed beads on the outside edge in the top portion of the piece. As shown in Figure 11, every other row of beads has a thread on the outside edge and it is desirable to tie two knots just above one of these beads. This way, the thread knots will lie between the beads and when the thread is passed up through additional beads to be concealed, the knot will pull snug against the bead and be less noticeable.

When the thread has been concealed in additional beads, clip it off close to the beads holding the scissors flat against the beadwork. It is suggested when concealing the thread, that after knotting, the thread be woven through beads on the inner part of the beadwork before it is clipped off to insure that the knot does not slip.

After completing this step, then thread the short beginning thread on the needle and tie off in the same manner as just described above: working the thread through a few beads, after knotting, to conceal it.

ADDING THREAD

When working on larger pieces of beadwork it may be necessary to add thread to the project. When the thread being used reaches about 6 to 8" in length, tie it off as when ending an earring as described earlier. To add a new length of Nymo, run the new thread through a few beads over to the edge of the beadwork and tie two knots using the same method as when the old thread was tied off. When the new thread is tied in, weave it up to the point where the beading was left off and continue as usual until the piece is complete. Figure 16 indicates the best places to tie off and/or add the new thread.

It is much easier, of course, to use Nymo of sufficient length to avoid having to add more thread.

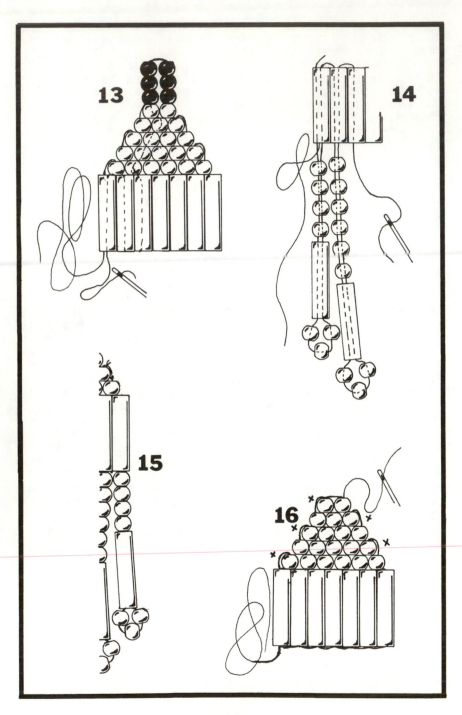

Graphs and Variation

The following pages contain graphs of designs for making beaded earrings using the techniques outlined in the preceding section.

The earring charts are placed in order of difficulty. The first are easy and simple, and those shown at the back of this section are more difficult. The most time consuming designs are those containing quills and those that have patterns in the bottom portion.

It is suggested that craftspersons who are not familiar with this type of beading begin with the simple charts and work toward the more difficult.

EXPLANATION OF GRAPHED STYLES

At the bottom of each graphed design there is a "style" noted. The following is a short explanation of each:

Regular Style refers to an earring, or necklace, in which the dangles (Phase III from the last section) taper in the regular "V" shape.

Tapered Dangle Style is an earring, or necklace, in which the dangle tapers in one direction. The dangle graduates from short on one side to long on the opposite side.

Because of the taper to one side, these earrings should be placed on the ear wires so that there is a left and right earring. Having the long side closest to the face seems to be more flattering in most cases.

Inverted Dangle Style refers to a piece in which the dangles taper to an inverted "V" shape. The longest dangles, in this case, will be on the outside.

Loop Style is an earring or necklace in which the dangles are made by looping the beads from one foundation bugle bead across to the

17

corresponding bugle opposite. For example, on a piece that is seven (7) bugle beads wide, the outside, and longest loop, would span from bugle #1 to bugle #7; the second loop would span from bugle #2 to bugle #6; the third loop would span from bugle #3 to bugle #5; and, the center would be a straight dangle from bugle #4 or there would be no dangle from #4, whichever is preferred.

Loop Style is not recommended for use on necklaces as they tend to catch on objects and break more easily than on earrings.

Bead & Quill Style is a piece in which porcupine quills are used in place of some of the beads in the dangles. A section on the preparation of quills is included in this section just prior to some of these charts.

Regular Style Bottom Design is an earring or necklace in which the dangles taper in the regular "V" shape, but also contains a definite "picture" design such as those used in loomwork beading, needlepoint, cross-stitch, or other charted designs.

Top or Bottom Design Styles refers to the portion of the beaded piece which contains the design. As noted above, the construction of the top piece was described in Phase II, and the bottom portion in Phase III.

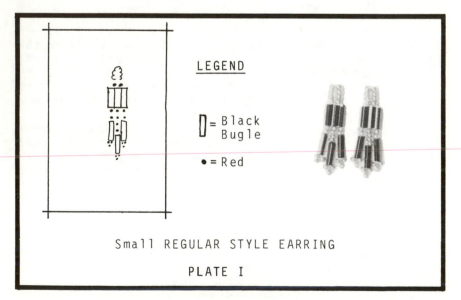

LEGEND

▯ = Black Bugle

• = Red

Small REGULAR STYLE EARRING

PLATE I

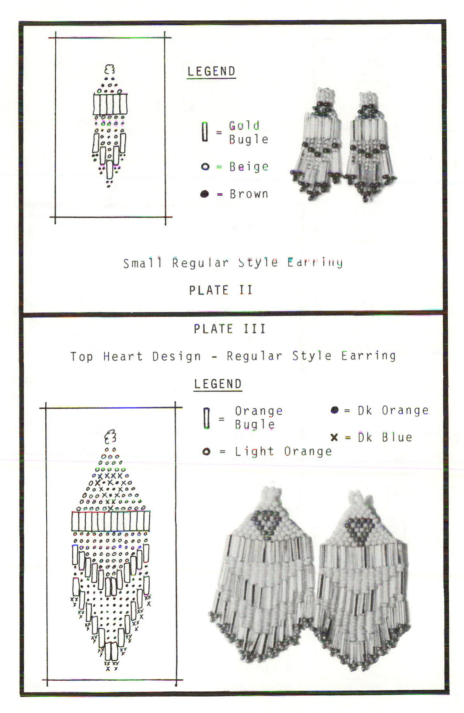

▯ = Gold Bugle

○ = Beige

● = Brown

Small Regular Style Earring

PLATE II

PLATE III

Top Heart Design - Regular Style Earring

LEGEND

▯ = Orange Bugle

○ = Light Orange

● = Dk Orange

✗ = Dk Blue

19

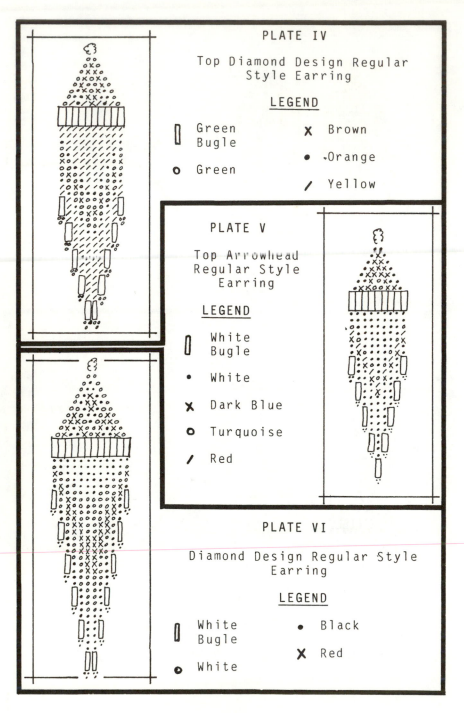

PLATE IV

Top Diamond Design Regular
Style Earring

LEGEND

▯ Green
  Bugle

✗ Brown

• Orange

o Green

/ Yellow

PLATE V

Top Arrowhead
Regular Style
Earring

LEGEND

▯ White
  Bugle

• White

✗ Dark Blue

o Turquoise

/ Red

PLATE VI

Diamond Design Regular Style
Earring

LEGEND

▯ White
  Bugle

• Black

✗ Red

o White

20

PLATE IV

PLATE V

PLATE VI

21

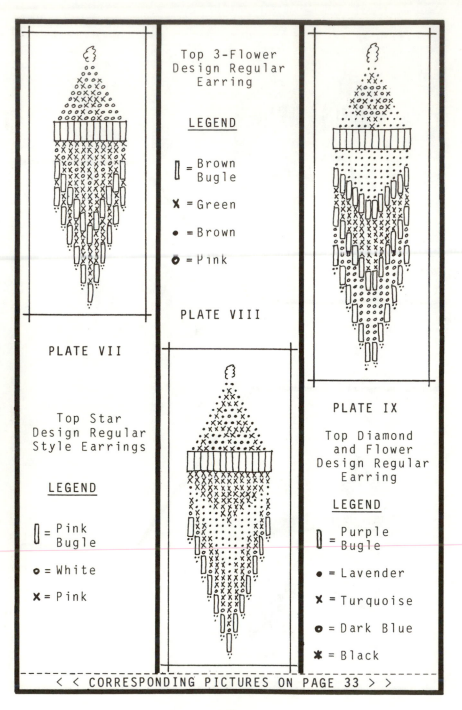

Top 3-Flower
Design Regular
Earring

LEGEND

▯ = Brown Bugle

✗ = Green

• = Brown

◉ = Pink

PLATE VIII

PLATE VII

Top Star
Design Regular
Style Earrings

LEGEND

▯ = Pink Bugle

◦ = White

✗ = Pink

PLATE IX

Top Diamond
and Flower
Design Regular
Earring

LEGEND

▯ = Purple Bugle

• = Lavender

✗ = Turquoise

◉ = Dark Blue

✱ = Black

< < CORRESPONDING PICTURES ON PAGE 33 > >

22

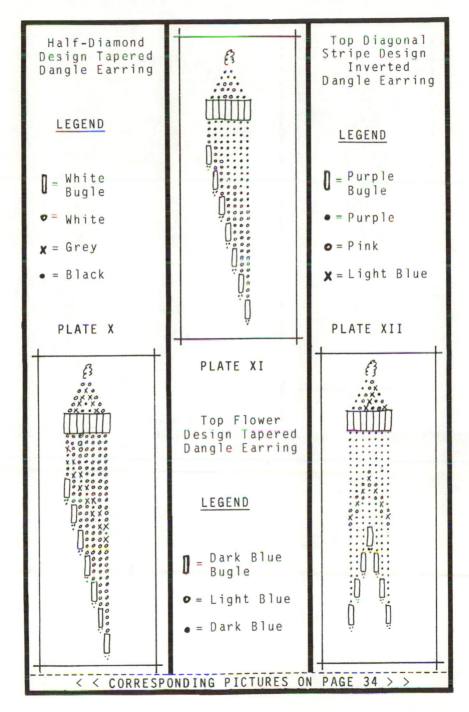

Half-Diamond
Design Tapered
Dangle Earring

LEGEND

▯ = White
    Bugle

♥ = White

✗ = Grey

● = Black

PLATE X

PLATE XI

Top Flower
Design Tapered
Dangle Earring

LEGEND

▯ = Dark Blue
    Bugle

♥ = Light Blue

● = Dark Blue

Top Diagonal
Stripe Design
Inverted
Dangle Earring

LEGEND

▯ = Purple
    Bugle

● = Purple

♥ = Pink

✗ = Light Blue

PLATE XII

< < CORRESPONDING PICTURES ON PAGE 34 > >

23

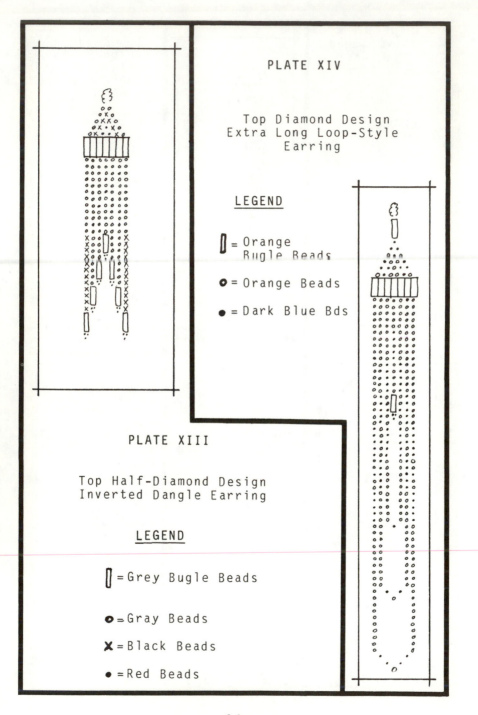

PLATE XIV

Top Diamond Design
Extra Long Loop-Style
Earring

LEGEND

▯ = Orange
     Bugle Beads

◐ = Orange Beads

● = Dark Blue Bds

PLATE XIII

Top Half-Diamond Design
Inverted Dangle Earring

LEGEND

▯ = Grey Bugle Beads

◐ = Gray Beads

X = Black Beads

● = Red Beads

24

‹ ‹ ‹ PLATE XIII › › ›

‹ ‹ ‹ PLATE XIV › › ›

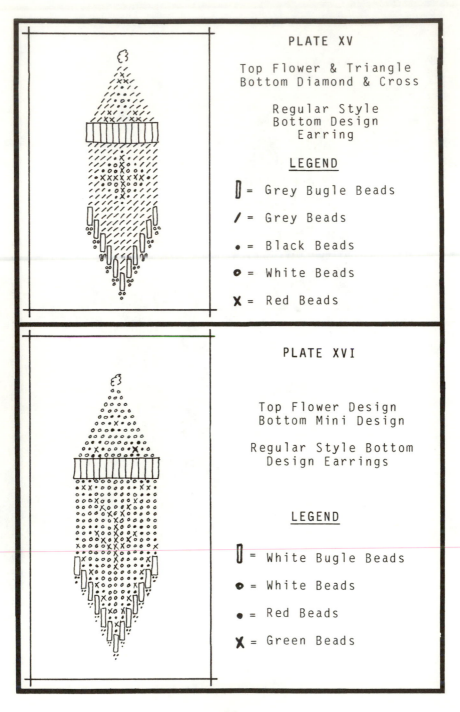

PLATE XV

Top Flower & Triangle
Bottom Diamond & Cross

Regular Style
Bottom Design
Earring

LEGEND

▯ = Grey Bugle Beads

/ = Grey Beads

• = Black Beads

◉ = White Beads

X = Red Beads

PLATE XVI

Top Flower Design
Bottom Mini Design

Regular Style Bottom
Design Earrings

LEGEND

▯ = White Bugle Beads

◉ = White Beads

• = Red Beads

X = Green Beads

26

27

Deon's Designs Originale Quilled Earrings

The following charted designs utilize porcupine quills in place of seed beads. Quills are available from most Indian craft supply houses or, in many parts of the country, it is possible to gather your own quills. In the latter case, the following may be helpful:

Porcupines have quills over most of their body, except for the stomach, and they are found below the long guard hair and mixed in with the short body hair. The best quills for making earrings are found on the back from the middle to the tail.

By being selective as the quills are pulled, it is possible to avoid getting a large amount of hair mixed in with the quills. The hair will have to be separated from the quills and by eliminating it to begin with, it makes sorting easier and quicker.

After the quills are pulled, they can be washed in a solution of 1 part liquid household cleaner and 3 parts water. Put this solution in a spray bottle and, after spreading the quills out on a surface that will drain, spray them liberally. After they have been covered completely with the solution, rinse them in warm water until the cleaner is rinsed off. Another method that works nicely is a plastic container that has a grater lid. Just make sure to use something the quills cannot slip through while washing them.

This procedure is to remove the natural body oils but if they are quite dirty, it may be necessary to wash them again.

If the quills are not going to be used immediately, after they have been washed and rinsed lay them on paper towels or newspaper to dry. The quills, when they are wet, will be flexible but will become firm again once they dry. Keep them separated so that they will dry faster. They may now be placed in an air tight container to keep them from becoming dusty. When it is time to use them, place the quills in warm water for a few minutes to soften them before following the next step.

If, however, the quills are to be used immediately, they are ready as soon as they have been rinsed as they can be cut without splitting when they are flexible. Select the quills largest in diameter and use a guage made from a piece of wire, or a toothpick, to cut a quantity of them to the same length, trimming off both ends. This can be done more accurately if the dark tip is clipped off first and then the length can be cut from the root end of the quill.

After the quills have been cut and have dried to a stage where they will not flatten out, select a long, fine pin with a large head. Quills are not hollow but have a pithy interior. The pin should be pushed through the very middle of this pithy material so that the hole made by the pin cannot be seen from the outside. The hole should be large enough to allow the beading needle to pass through readily without causing the thread to fray or the needle to bend or break. The quills may be cut to any length desired, but must be at least one-half ($\frac{1}{2}$") inch shorter than the beading needle used when making the earrings. If they are longer, it is impossible to pull the needle and thread through them.

By doing several quills at the same time and keeping them in a separate container, it will speed up the beading process when making this style.

- - - - - - - - - -

Variations may be made of any of the graphed designs shown in this section by using other kinds of beads, dentallium shells, Russian olive seeds, etc. Simply by changing the colors involved in any of the designs shown, it is possible to change the appearance greatly.

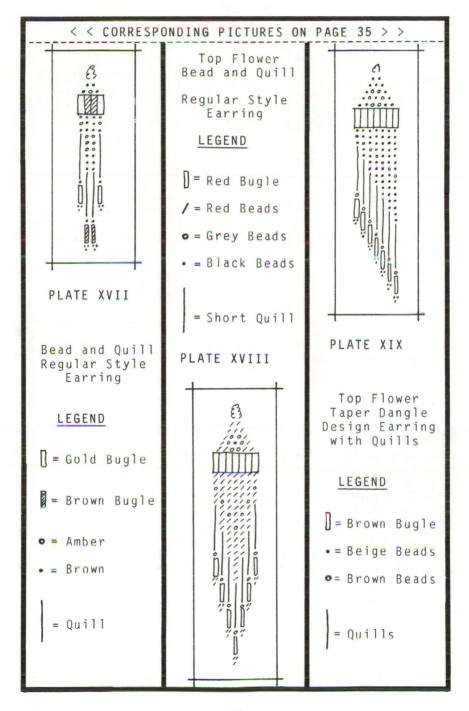

PLATE XVII

Top Flower
Bead and Quill

Regular Style
Earring

LEGEND

▯ = Red Bugle

∕ = Red Beads

☉ = Grey Beads

• = Black Beads

∣ = Short Quill

PLATE XVIII

PLATE XIX

Bead and Quill
Regular Style
Earring

LEGEND

▯ = Gold Bugle

▨ = Brown Bugle

☉ = Amber

• = Brown

∣ = Quill

Top Flower
Taper Dangle
Design Earring
with Quills

LEGEND

▯ = Brown Bugle

• = Beige Beads

☉ = Brown Beads

∣ = Quills

31

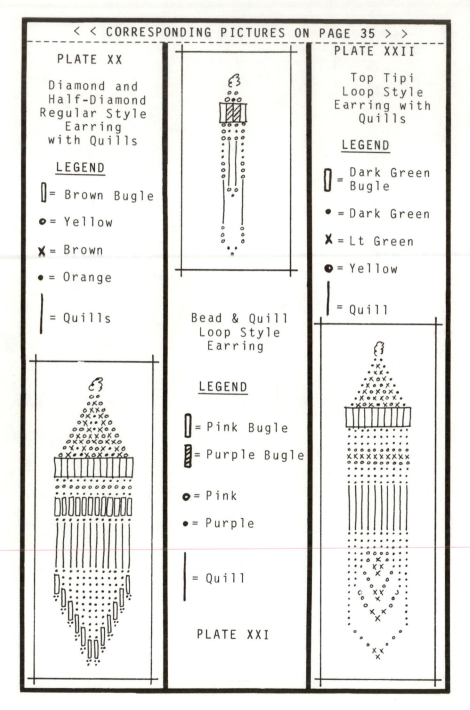

PLATE XX

Diamond and
Half-Diamond
Regular Style
Earring
with Quills

LEGEND

▯ = Brown Bugle

◉ = Yellow

✗ = Brown

● = Orange

❘ = Quills

PLATE XXII

Top Tipi
Loop Style
Earring with
Quills

LEGEND

▯ = Dark Green Bugle

● = Dark Green

✗ = Lt Green

◉ = Yellow

❘ = Quill

Bead & Quill
Loop Style
Earring

LEGEND

▯ = Pink Bugle

▨ = Purple Bugle

◉ = Pink

● = Purple

❘ = Quill

PLATE XXI

PLATE V11

PLATE VIII

PLATE IX

- -

CORRESPONDING GRAPHS ON PAGE 22

PLATE X

PLATE XI

PLATE XII

CORRESPONDING GRAPHS ON PAGE 23

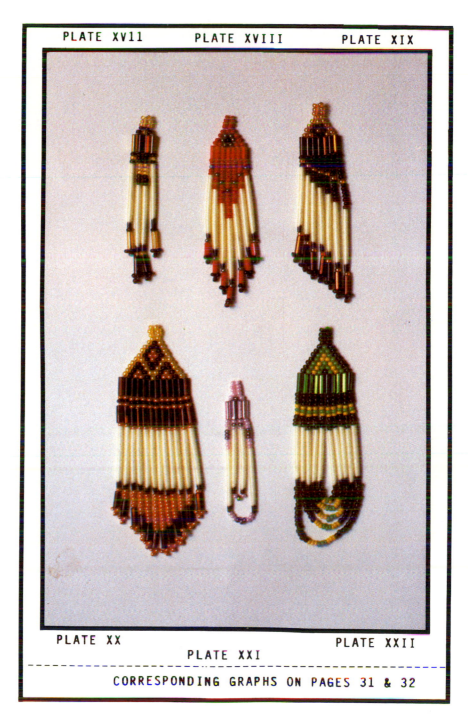

PLATE XX   PLATE XXII
PLATE XXI

CORRESPONDING GRAPHS ON PAGES 31 & 32

PLATE XXV

PLATE XXIV

CORRESPONDING GRAPHS ON PAGE 41

Necklace & Loop

All of the necklaces in this section may be made with the following recommended materials:

      1 bobbin "nymo" thread size A or O
      1 package 15/° beading needles
      1 pair small sharp scissors
      1 hank bugle beads - either size 3/°
          or 2/°*
      1 hank seed beads - either size 11/°
          or 12/°*
      1 hank contrasting color seed beads -
          either size 11/° or 12/°*
      ----
      * - see "Introduction" for correct
      combination of seed and bugle beads.

Making the body of the necklace is done by following the steps in the first section, Phases I through IV. As shown in the following charted graphs, the techniques are the same but they may be made larger.

In order to attach the body of the necklace to the necklace chain, it is necessary to construct a "hanging loop strip." The same procedure is used to make the hanging loop strip as you used for making the top portion of the beadwork (Phase II), with one exception, which comes in attaching the second bead of each row.

The first bead of each row of the hanging loop strip will be put in place in the usual manner used in Phase II of the earring section as shown in Figure 17. The two dark beads in all of the following figures indicate the top row of the beadwork in the necklace piece.

After the first bead has been put in place in the usual manner, string a second bead on the thread and pass the needle under the thread lying on the outside edge of the bead in the preceding

37

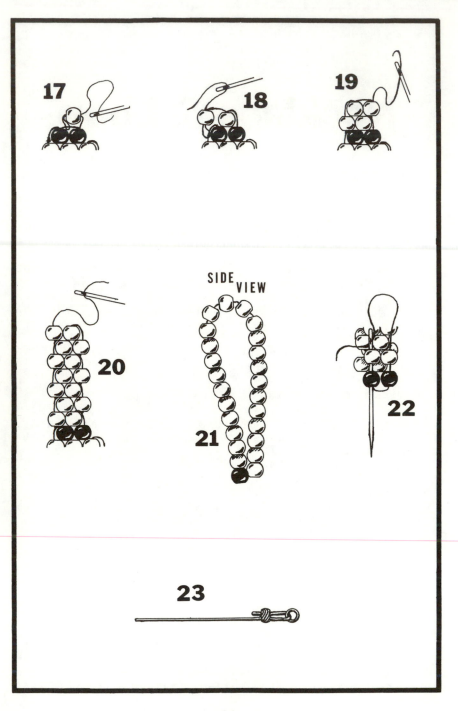

17

18

19

20

SIDE VIEW

21

22

23

row as shown in Figure 18. The remaining rows will be put on using this same technique (Figure 19).

Figure 20 shows seven rows of the hanging loop strip; note the "zig-zag" pattern that is formed.

For an average necklace, the hanging loop strip will contain approximately twenty-four (24) rows of beadwork, two beads wide. This length will allow almost any size beads used on the bead necklace chain (explained in the next section) to easily pass through the hanging loop when it is completed.

To form the hanging loop from the 24 row strip now constructed, fold the strip over until the two beads in the last row of the strip are directly in front of the two beads in the top row of the necklace piece. Figure 21 is a side view of the loop now formed. Fasten the hanging loop by passing the needle down through the bead on the top row of the necklace body (Figure 22), then up through the other bead at the top of the necklace body, up through the corresponding bead at the end of the hanging loop strip and repeat this procedure two or three times for reinforcement.

You are now ready to work the thread down through the necklace body in order to add the dangles (Phase III), or if the thread is too short, tie it off, and tie in a longer one (as explained in the earring section above - Page 15).

- - - - - - - - - -

It should be noted that this section of instructions, for making the hanging loop, are written with the thread emerging from the bead on the right hand side of the top row in the necklace body. However, if a necklace is made in which the thread is coming from the bead on the left side, the only difference is that the first row will be worked from left to right rather than right to left as in the instructions. The number of bugle beads contained in the foundation determine from which of the two top beads the thread will emerge. Using an uneven number of bugle beads will place the thread on the right hand side of the top row; whereas, an even number of bugles will place the thread on the left side. In either case, the final results will be the same.

Also, if the body of the necklace is

particuliarly large (e.g., the rose pattern
pictured on the front cover), it will help make the
body more sturdy by running additional thread
through the beads as done when going down from the
top to the dangles.
   The following are graphs and photos of some
necklace bodies that may be made from these
instructions:

PLATE XXIII

3 Flower
Design
Regular
Style with
Quills

LEGEND

▮ = Lavender
     Bugle

● = Lavender

X = Purple

❙ = Quill

40

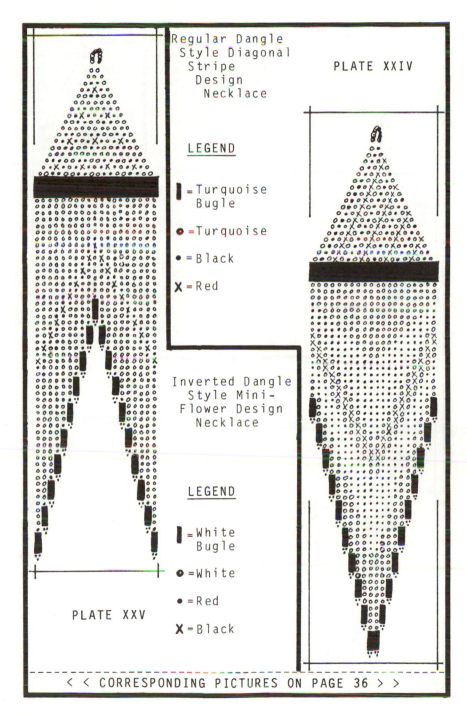

Regular Dangle
Style Diagonal
    Stripe
    Design
   Necklace

PLATE XXIV

LEGEND

▌ = Turquoise
      Bugle

◉ = Turquoise

● = Black

✕ = Red

Inverted Dangle
Style Mini-
Flower Design
    Necklace

LEGEND

▌ = White
     Bugle

◉ = White

● = Red

✕ = Black

PLATE XXV

< < CORRESPONDING PICTURES ON PAGE 36 > >

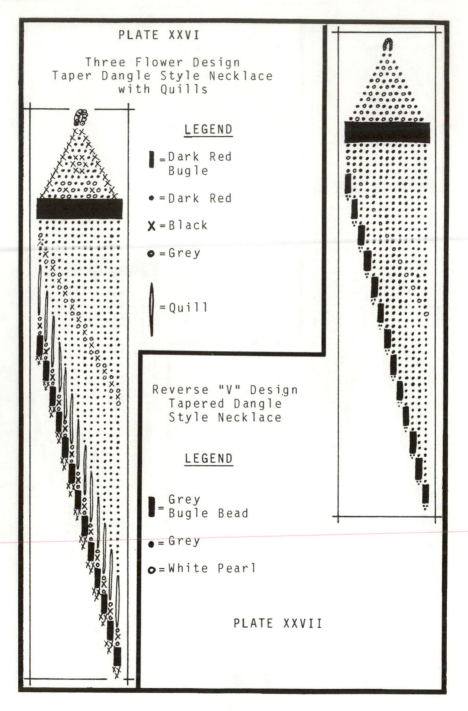

PLATE XXVI

Three Flower Design
Taper Dangle Style Necklace
with Quills

LEGEND

▮ = Dark Red
    Bugle

● = Dark Red

X = Black

◉ = Grey

◇ = Quill

Reverse "V" Design
Tapered Dangle
Style Necklace

LEGEND

▮ = Grey
    Bugle Bead

● = Grey

○ = White Pearl

PLATE XXVII

42

PLATE XXVI   PLATE XXVII

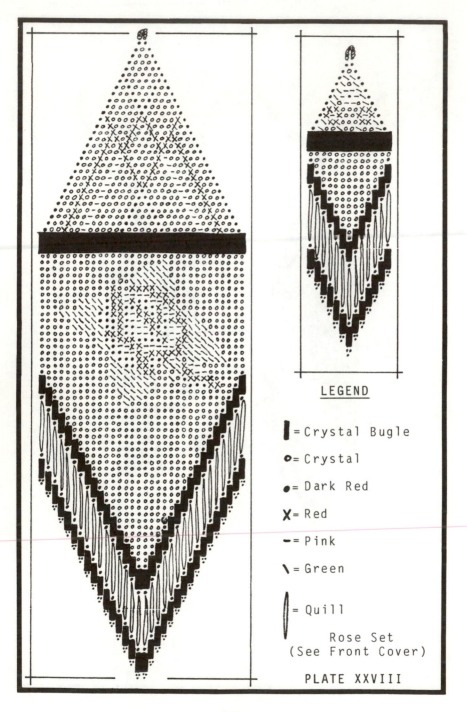

LEGEND

▋ = Crystal Bugle

๐ = Crystal

● = Dark Red

X = Red

━ = Pink

╲ = Green

⬭ = Quill

Rose Set
(See Front Cover)

PLATE XXVIII

44

Necklace Bead Chain

In order to secure the necklace around the neck, it is necessary to make a "chain" in the following manner:

Recommended Materials Needed

1 Spool Size 12 Tigertail Wire
2 Crimp beads (either gold or silver colors)
1 Pair small needle nose pliers
1 Spring-type necklace clamp
1 6mm Jump Ring (either gold or silver)

First determine the desired length of the necklace chain. An average length for a finished chain is approximately eighteen (18") inches. To allow for attaching the crimp beads, add about two (2") inches to the desired finished length. For example, to make an 18" chain, the tiger tail should be cut to approximately twenty (20") inches.

After the tigertail has been cut to the desired length, slip a crimp bead over one end and position it about one (1") inch from the end. Put a jump ring over the same end following the crimp bead. Now take the short end of the tigertail over the jump ring and through the crimp bead to form a loop; allow the jump ring to hang free in the loop just formed. When the loop is adjusted, squeeze the crimp bead closed with the pliers (See Figure 23 for a view of the finished loop).

Now string the beads on the tiger tail, in any desired pattern, to within approximately one inch from the end of the tigertail. The photos shown in this book will give some good examples of patterns that may be used but the variations are endless.

When the pattern is acceptable, slip the other crimp bead over the 1" end of the tigertail. Now put the tigertail through the small ring of the necklace clamp, fold the tigertail over and go back through the crimp bead and close it with the pliers. This step finishes the bead chain.

Attach the necklace portion to the bead chain by sliding either end of the chain through the hanging loop.

It is important to have the two halves of the necklace chain correspond in pattern by having the same number of beads on each side. If there is to be a "center pattern" that will vary from the rest of the chain, it is recommended that you begin the chain by putting the center pattern on the tigertail first, sliding it to the middle and then add one pattern of beads at a time, working first on one side, then on the other until approximately 1" remains on both ends. Then add the crimp beads, jump ring and necklace clasp as before.

The only difficult part of the "center pattern technique" is keeping the beads from sliding off of one end while the loop is being made on the opposite end. The open end may be secured with an "alligator clip," by holding it in your teeth or by finding a "helping hand."

Keep in mind that the possible variations that may be used in making the necklace chain are almost unlimited and beads made of glass, wood, ceramic, metal, etc., may be used. The only requirement is that they have a hole big enough to allow the tigertail to be used, and that the bead be small enough to go through the hanging loop.

Figures 24 and 25, on the next two pages, shows some of the necklace chains that can be made.

FIGURE 24

FIGURE 25

Earring Styles

The following pages describe a variety of earrings that may be made following the instructions given. By combining different styles, almost any kind of earring may be created.

The kind of stringing material will also affect the appearance of the finished earrings. Tigertail tends to be very stiff, nylon beading wire (or fishing leader) is less rigid, and nymo beading thread is very flexible.

LOOP STYLE QUILL EARRING

Recommended Materials Needed

1 Bobbin Nymo thread (size A of O)
1 Hank Seed Beads (either Size 11/°
    or 12/° - color "A")
1 Hank Seed Beads (same size in
complimentary color - "B")
1 Small leather scrap
8 Porcupine quills
2 Earwires

Tools Needed

1 Size 16 beading needle
1 Pair small, sharp pointed scissors
1 Leather punch (optional, but help-
    ful. Scissors may be used.)

First, prepare porcupine quills as described before. Then, from the leather, punch (or cut) a small circle (or square) approximately ¼" in diameter. Thread the beading needle with a piece of Nymo approximately 36" long, pull needle to middle and make a knot using both ends of the thread. Do Not cut off the ends of the knot thread.

Begin by pushing the needle down through the leather disc. Make this "hole" about half way between the middle and the outside of the disc. Pull the thread completely through the leather so that the knot is snug against it.

Then begin beading in this order: 3 beads of color A, 3 beads of color B, 3 beads A, 1 quill (place white end on needle first), 3 beads A, 3 beads B, 3 beads A, 3 beads B, 3 beads A, 3 beads B, 3 beads A, 1 quill (place dark tip on needle first), 3 beads color A, 3 beads color B, and 3 beads color A.

This forms the first loop, so now pass the needle up through the leather piece again, this time halfway between center and the other side of the disc. Pull the thread all the way through so that the beads and quills are resting against each other, but not so tight that they are crowded.

Now string six (6) beads of color A on the thread and go back down **almost** through the first hole as shown in Figure 26. Then repeat the beading sequence noted above to form a second loop. When this is complete, take the needle up through the leather disc almost through the second hole.

At this stage it is possible to adjust the beads/quills so that they are niether too loose or tight. When the earring is just right, remove the needle and tie the excess thread to the excess knot thread in a small, tight knot. The knot should be small enough to be hidden under the beads that form the 6 bead loop. Now, cut off excess thread. A small spot of craft glue may be used on the nylon knot, but this isn't usually necessary. The earwires are placed on the small loop between the 3rd and 4th beads.

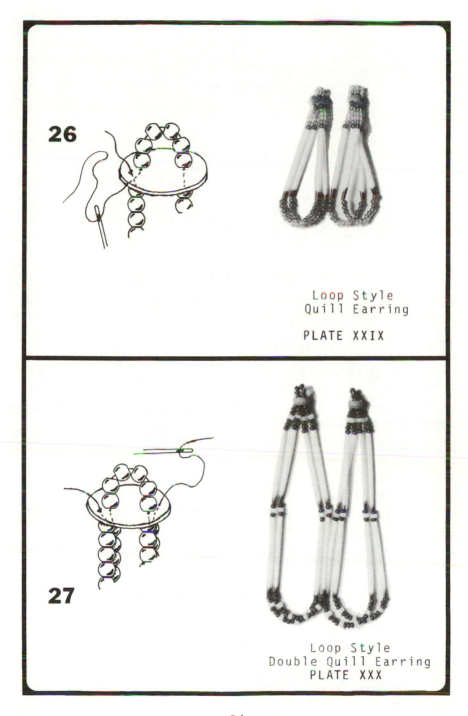

26

Loop Style
Quill Earring

PLATE XXIX

27

Loop Style
Double Quill Earring
PLATE XXX

51

LOOP STYLE DOUBLE QUILL EARRING

Recommended Materials Needed

1 Bobbin Nymo thread (size A of 0)
1 Hank Seed Beads (either Size 11/°
    or 12/° - color "A")
1 Hank Seed Beads (same size in
complimentary color - "B")
1 Small leather scrap
16 Porcupine quills
2 Earwires

Tools Needed

1 Size 16 beading needle
1 Pair small, sharp pointed scissors
1 Leather punch (optional, but help-
    ful. Scissors may be used.)

This style earring is simply a variation of the last one shown and is given as an example of some of the possibilities using similiar techniques.

The initial steps for this style are exactly as noted for the last style: First, prepare porcupine quills as described before. Then punch (or cut) a small circle (or square) of leather approximately ¼" in diameter. Thread the beading needle with a piece of Nymo approximately 42" long, pull needle to middle and place a small knot using both ends of the thread. **Do Not cut off the ends of the knot thread.**

Begin by pushing the needle down through the leather disc. Make this "hole" about half way between the middle and the outside of the disc. Pull the thread completely through the leather so that the knot is snug against it.

Then begin stringing the beads as follows: 3 beads color A, 1 bead color B, 3 beads color A, 1 quill (place white end on needle first), 1 bead A, 1 bead B, 1 bead A, 1 quill (place white end on needle first), 3 beads color A, 1 bead B, 3 beads A, 1 bead color B, 3 beads color A, 1 bead B, 3 beads A, 1 bead B, 3 beads A, 1 quill (place black tip on needle first), 1 bead A, 1 bead B, 1 bead A, 1 quill (place black tip on needle first), 3 beads color A, 1 bead color B, and 3 beads color A.

This forms the first loop, so now pass the needle up through the leather piece again, this time halfway between center and the other side of the disc. Pull the thread all the way through so that the beads and quills are resting against each other, but not so tight that they are crowded.

Now string six (6) beads of color A on the thread and go back down **almost** through the first hole. Then repeat the beading sequence noted above to form a second loop. When this is complete, take the needle up through the leather disc almost through the second hole.

At this stage (Figure 27) it is possible to adjust the beads/quills so that they are neither too loose or tight. When the earring is just right, remove the needle and tie the excess thread to the excess knot thread in a small, tight knot. The knot should be small enough to be hidden under the beads that form the 6 bead loop. Now, cut off excess thread. A **small** spot of craft glue may be used on the nylon knot, but this isn't usually necessary. The earwires are placed on the small loop between the 3rd and 4th beads.

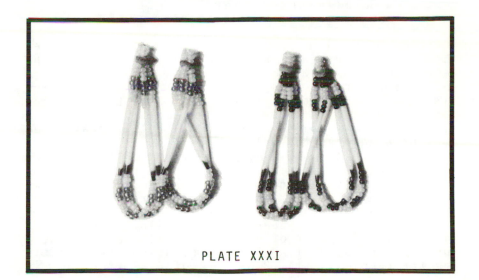

PLATE XXXI

53

TIN CONE, QUILL AND BEAD EARRING

Recommended Materials Needed

1 Bobbin Beading Thread - Nymo size A
    or 0
1 Hank Seed Beads - either size 11/°
    or size 12/° (color "A")
1 Hank Seed Beads - same size in
    complimentary color "B"
6 Size 10/° seed beads - any size
    that will not slip through the
    small end of a tin cone. One
    bead for each dangle on earring.
    Color is not important.
8 Tin, Aluminium or Silver Cones in
    $\frac{3}{4}$" to 1" length
6 Porcupine Quills - approx $\frac{1}{2}$" long
2 Eye-pins or 18 gauge florist wire.

Necessary tools

1 Beading Needle - English Size 15 or
    Japanese Size 16
1 Needle-nose pliers - small craft
    size with wire cutter jaws.

Prepare the porcupine quills as explained before. Then tie one size 10/° seed bead to the end of a length of thread using two or three overhand knots. This dangle will give you a better idea of the length of thread that will be suitable, but it is best to begin with about 18" so that there will be working room. A spot of craft glue may be used over the nylon knot if desired.

Thread the needle on this Nymo strand and string the tied bead through the cone placing the larger end of the cone on the needle first as shown in Figure 28. Pull the thread through until the bead is snug into the top of the cone.

Then, string beads in the following sequence: 4 beads color A, 4 of color B, 4 color A, 4 of B, 2 of A, 2 of B, 2 of A, 1 quill (placing the dark tip on the needle first), 2 of A, 2 of B, 2 of A.

Secure the thread, by tying two or three knots, to the loop in the eyepin (or make a small loop in one end of the florist wire with the needle nose pliers and secure to this). Clip off the excess thread (and there will be alot of it) close to the knot. Add a **drop** of glue if desired.

Following the instructions in the last two paragraphs, make two more dangles. Make sure that all three of the dangles are secured to the eye pin.

Now position a cone over the top of the eye pin (large end first), as shown in Figure 29, and pull eye pin through the cone until a few beads are slightly inside of the cone.

At this stage, use the needle-nose pliers to make a small loop in the eye pin just above the top of the cone (see Figure 30). The ear wires are attached to these top loops.

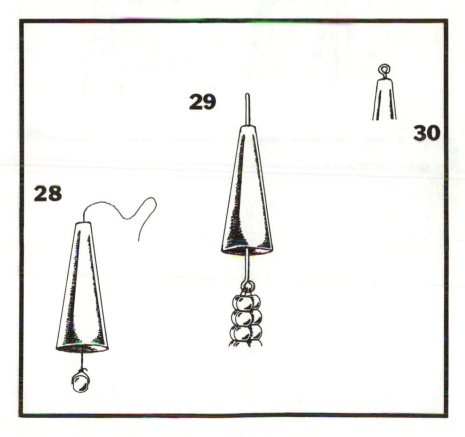

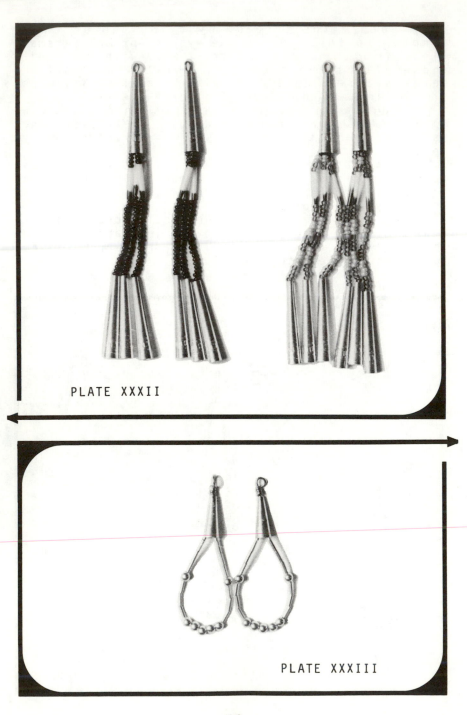

PLATE XXXII

PLATE XXXIII

HEISHI (Liquid Silver) EARRING

Recommended Materials Needed

 2 Sterling Silver Cones
 2 Eye-Pins or 18 gauge florist wire
 1 Nylon Beading Wire
 2 Abalone Shells
 4 Shell Heishi
 2 Crimp Beads
 2 10/° Seed Beads
20 Sterling Silver Heishi ("Liquid Silver")

Necessary Tools

 2 Needle-nose pliers - May be done with one
    pair, but will be easier with two.

Following these instructions it is possible to construct any number of variations of heishi-style earrings and necklaces. Simply by substituting hollow sterling silver balls for the shell heishi in this example will result in very attractive, yet different, earrings.

Begin with a length of nylon beading wire (or 8-10 pound test fishing leader) about 20" long. This length will be far more than needed, but will allow stringing the heishi without losing it off the open end. On this nylon, string 5 silver hieshi, 1 shell heishi, 2 silver heishi, 1 shell heishi, 3 silver heishi, 1 abalone piece, 3 silver heishi, 1 shell heishi, 2 silver heishi, 1 shell heishi and 5 silver heishi. Then place the eye-pin on the nylon and let it slip down over the silver heishi.

Put both ends of the nylon through one of the crimp beads and, holding the crimp bead, pull the nylon until the crimp bead is **almost** touching the tops of the silver heishi. If the nylon is too taut it will distort the shape of the earring.

Now hold the nylon just above the crimp bead

and, with the needle-nose pliers, crush the bead to hold the nylon tight. There will be a great deal of excess nylon and this may now be cut off.

Slip the eye-pin up over the crimp bead and when it is in position, use the pliers to crush it against the crimp bead as shown in Figure 31.

Now place the silver cone over the top of the eye-pin, large end first, and down snug against the crimp bead. There are a number of variations that can be used at the top of the eye-pin to form a loop. One was explained before with the "tin cone" earrings on page 55 and if this technique is used, a portion of the eye-pin will probably have to be cut off and discarded. However, a more difficult variation can be much more attractive.

With one pair of needle-nose pliers hold the eye pin leaving approximately 3/8" between the bottom of the pliers and the top of the silver cone. Bend the eye-pin over the nose of the pliers to form the loop and then, with the other pliers, wrap the remainder of the pin around the exposed portion above the silver cone. In order to be attractive, this technique will require some patience and practice (see Figure 32).

Using the methods explained on pages 45-46, matching necklaces may be made to construct some very attractive heishi sets.

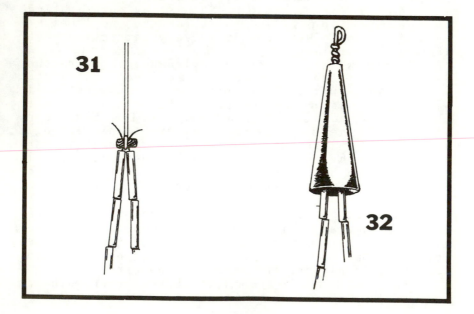

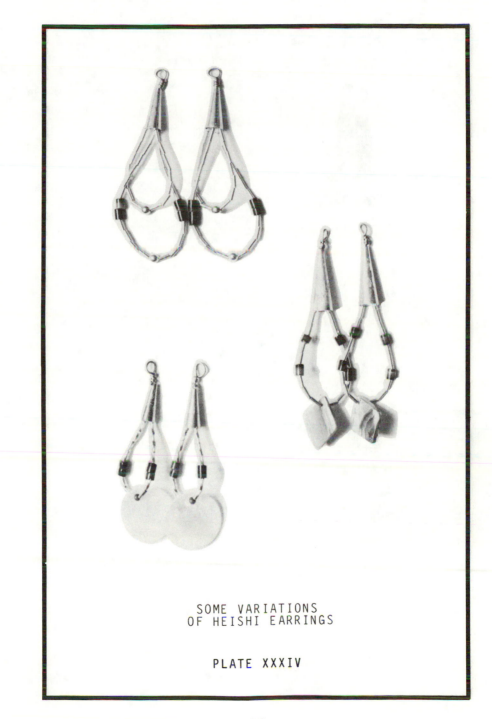

SOME VARIATIONS
OF HEISHI EARRINGS

PLATE XXXIV

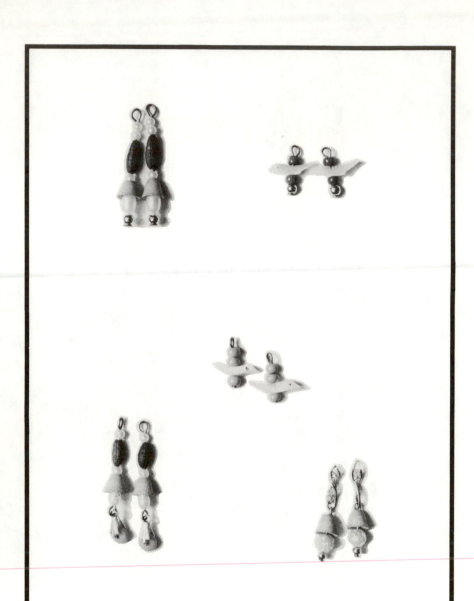

PICTURES OF SOME OF THE EARRINGS
THAT MAY BE MADE FOLLOWING THE TECHNIQUES
OUTLINED IN THIS SECTION
(Note the use of headpins in place of eyepins)

PLATE XXXV

Peyote Stitch

Earrings

The Peyote Stitch may be used on any round or irregular shaped object and is a natural for earrings. (For a complete explanation of general beadwork using this technique, please see **The Techniques of North American Indian Beadwork** by Monte Smith.)

When using this stitch: First, using uniform beads is an absolute necessity. Second, for the first two or three pair of earrings, the work will go more smoothly if the body of the earring is made around a small dowel covered with leather or felt as shown in PLATE XXXVI (lower left-hand, Page 63). This will provide a base for the beadwork. After a few pairs have been made, and the technique mastered, make the earring body around a plastic straw that can be removed **before** adding the top and dangles (lower right-hand, Page 63 and those on Page 64). Further, earring patterns may be charted in advance on a special "peyote stitch graph paper" that is available from most Indian craft supply stores. Finally, use a size "A" or "0" thread and a small needle (13 or 15) as it is necessary to go through each bead twice or more times.

To begin, start with one row of beads as shown in Figure 33. The beads should have a space one-bead-wide between each bead. The second row (Figure 34) is then added between the beads of the first row. Each successive row is beaded into place in the same way forming a pattern as shown in Figure 35. The number of rows needed depends upon personal preference.

When the last row is in place, this will become the bottom of the earring and the dangles are

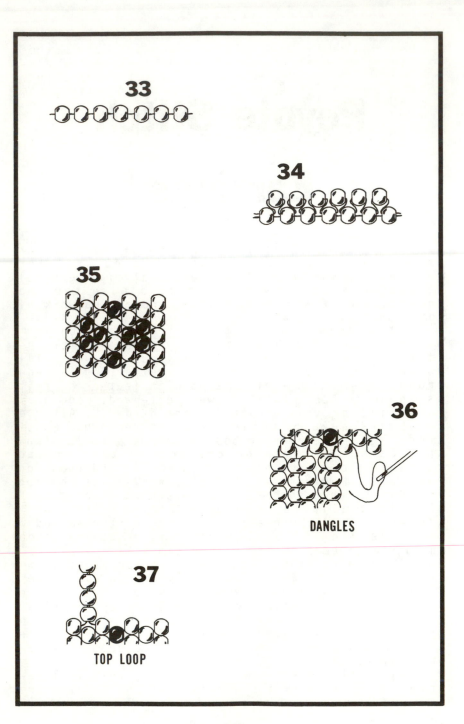

33

34

35

36

DANGLES

37

TOP LOOP

put into place. Simply take the needle through one of the bottom beads, string the beads, quills, or whatever on the thread that is desired on the dangle and then go through the next (or every other) bottom bead. String an equal amount of material to form the next dangle (Figure 36). The thread at the end of the last dangle should go through the same bead as the beginning of the first dangle.

With the thread from the last dangle properly placed through the first "dangle" bead used, thread the needle up through the peyote stitch body of the earring until it emerges from one of the top beads. As shown in Figure 37, place an even number of beads on the thread (usually either six or eight) and then take the needle through the top bead directly across the body from where you started. Pull the thread to form a loop and then go back through the beads in the loop and into the body of the earring.

The final step is to take the needle and thread back into the body of the earring and tie off the thread using a small knot and hiding it between, and in back of, the beads.

This stitch requires some practice but is not too difficult to do correctly. With a little exposure, many short cuts will become evident.

PLATE XXXVI

PLATE XXXVII

Designing Earrings

In order to design your own earrings, they should first be charted on graph paper which is used as a guide. Almost any kind of graph paper may be used, but paper with a scale of 13 squares per inch will give you a graph that is more accurate to the actual finished size of the beadwork piece.

The final design is best charted using fine-point felt tip markers in assorted colors that represent the bead colors being used.

When graphing designs, remember that in the top portion of the Deon Originale-type earrings, each row of beadwork will contain one less bead than the preceding row, including the foundation row of bugle beads. Therefore, when charting designs it should be noted that the bugle beads are drawn using one space wide and three spaces high to represent each bead. The first row of beadwork directly above the bugle bead foundation will move in one-half space, and therefore the first seed bead row, and every other row above it, will be shown on the lines of the graph paper. This is shown on the charts shown in this book. The second seed bead row, and every other row above it, will be shown using the spaces of the graph paper. Again, this should be clear by looking at the designs shown throughout.

When graphing a design of your own, it is advisable to chart the inner design portion first (for example, the rose, flower, etc.), and to work in pencil until the design is satisfactory.

When the design portion has been completed, the number of bugle beads **and** the number of rows of beads is determined by the size of the design. It is very important, therefore, that the design be charted first. When this is complete, the outer edge beads may be charted in.

Throughout this book, all of the beads have been charted in. It may be less complicated and easier to follow, however, if only the inner design and the outer edge beads are charted.

Another consideration that is important in this type of beadwork is that the beads in the top portion of the earring (Phase II) run diagonally and not vertical, or straight up and down. Therefore, when considering designs that require straight vertical lines, it may be best to use them on the dangle (Phase III) portion of the earrings. Please refer to charts and photos of "Bottom Design Style" earrings.

Another use of the graph paper is to make variations of designs. For example, the "Rose Design" earrings that appear on the front cover of this book is charted on Page 44, but a variation of that design has been used on a lamp shade as seen on Page 67. By using graph paper, and referring to Page 44, it is simply a matter of time to chart the design used on the lamp shade fringe. Further, the design used on earrings may be expanded for use on the necklace portion of any of the earring graphs found in this book. Or, conversely, a necklace design may be contracted to make earrings.

When an earring has been completed, it is easy to make a record of the colors, style and design by simply gluing a bead of the appropriate color directly onto the graph paper next to the design. If the beads are glued to the paper in the order in which they were used, no further notation will be necessary. For example, bugles, background, main color, secondary color, etc. Then additional pieces of different colors using the same design can be recorded in the same way on the same sheet of graph paper. This procedure also utilizes less storage space and less graph paper.

Keeping your design sheets in a folder will help protect them and keep them in order for easy reference. Also, subject divider pages will help to keep them in catagories; i.e., necklaces, earrings, quill earrings, etc. according to style, type or design.

These same instructions, of course, may be used for earrings, necklaces or even lamp shades!

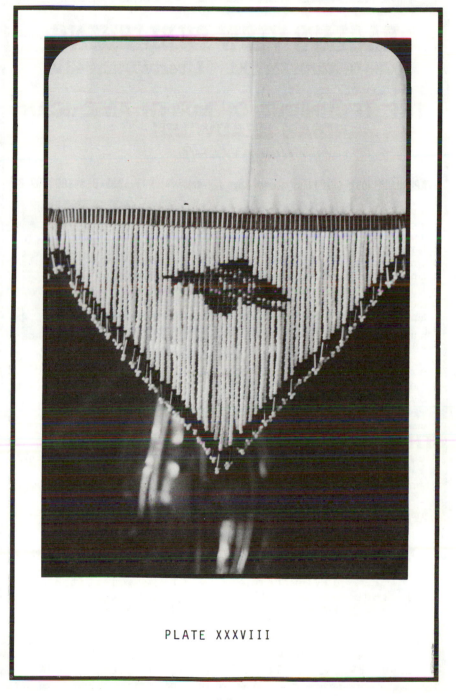

PLATE XXXVIII